Nod of Knowing

Nod of Knowing

J. Pittman McGehee

LITERARY PRESS
LAMAR UNIVERSITY

ISBN: 978-1-942956-56-3
Library of Congress Control Number: 2018948114

Cover by Merrilee McGehee

Lamar University Literary Press
Beaumont, Texas

Acknowledgments

Once again, Jerry Craven, Press Director for Lamar University Press, is responsible for this our third book together. Jerry is a great asset for and friend to Texas poetry. Katherine Hoerth is to be acknowledged for her very professional editing and typesetting. Jazz Jaeschke transcribed the poems from my handwritten poetry journal, to the typed. Her tireless contribution made this book possible. Finally, I offer thanks and praise to my daughter-in-law, Merrilee McGehee, for her design of this beautiful cover. She is an exceptional artist. I acknowledge all the above for creating this piece of work.

Recent Poetry from Lamar University Literary Press

Bobby Aldridge, *An Affair of the Stilled Heart*
Michael Baldwin, *Lone Star Heart, Poems of a Life in Texas*
Roberto Bonazzi, *Awakened By Surprise*
David Bowles, *Flower, Song, Dance: Aztec and Mayan Poetry*
Jerry Bradley and Ulf Kirchdorfer, editors, *The Great American Wise Ass Poetry Anthology*
Matthew Brennan, *One Life*
Mark Busby, *Through Our Times*
Paul Christensen, *The Jack of Diamonds Is a Hard Card to Play*
Stan Crawford, *Resisting Gravity*
Chip Dameron, *Waiting for an Etcher*
Glover Davis, *My Cap of Darkness*
William Virgil Davis, *The Bones Poems*
Jeffrey DeLotto, *Voices Writ in Sand*
Chris Ellery, *Elder Tree*
Alan Gann, *That's Entertainment*
Larry Griffin, *Cedar Plums*
Michelle Hartman, *Irony and Irrelevance*
Katherine Hoerth, *Goddess Wears Cowboy Boots*
Michael Jennings, *Crossings: A Record of Travel*
Gretchen Johnson, *A Trip Through Downer, Minnesota*
Ulf Kirchdorfer, *Chewing Green Leaves*
Janet McCann, *The Crone at the Casino*
Jim McGarrah, *A Balancing Act*
Laurence Musgrove, *One Kind of Recording*
Godspower Oboido, *Wandering Feet on Pebbled Shores*
Carol Coffee Reposa, *Underground Musicians*
Jan Seale, *The Parkinson Poems*
Steven Schroeder, *the moon, not the finger, pointing*
Glen Sorestad, *Hazards of Eden*
Vincent Spina, *The Sumptuous Hills of Gulfport*
W.K. Stratton, *Ranchero Ford/ Dying in Red Dirt Country*
Wally Swist, *Invocation*
Loretta Diane Walker, *Desert Light*
Dan Williams, *Past Purgatory, a Distant Paradise*
Jonas Zdanys, *Three White Horses*

For information on these and other Lamar University Literary Press books go to www.Lamar.edu/literarypress

"We cannot, therefore, afford to be indifferent to the poets, since in their principal works and deepest inspirations they create from the very depths of the collective unconscious, voicing aloud what others only dream."

—C. G. Jung

CONTENTS

Shutter

My morning ritual is to open
the bedroom shutter to view
the day. The shutter's purpose
is to shut. But it also has the
ability to open and reveal.
Must be a metaphor in there some-
where. That which shuts up or
down, may reveal, when opened
to the light. Today the ritual re-
vealed a gray day. Low clouds
shut out the Sun. There were
circles of water where a brief
shower wet the earth. The
blossoms from the tree fell
in the puddle making a mirror
of purple petals in a pedestrian
street scene. I looked for
Williams' "red wheelbarrow."
I shudder to think how much I
would miss if I abandoned my
morning ritual of opening
the shutter.

Gift of a Second Son

So when the time was
right we were given the
gift of a second son. Blonde
hair, sky blue eyes, old
soul, keen sense of humor
and a presence of the Presence.

Today he is forty-one. He
has created for us a second
son's second family.
Full of his wit, wisdom,
and unbounded eros, the

passionate desire to
connect, relate and create.
His appeal is most appealing.
His humility is grounding.
His sense of the other is
fulfilling. It is J's

Day. The Day the Creator
smiled on us with the
gift of a child of God.

God's name be praised!

Projection

Three women in a booth ex-
changing gifts. Pretty bags
with colorful tissue hold gifts
and cute cards. I love to make

stories of public scenes. These
women were sorority sisters.
They have a ritual of wine and
lunch on one another's birthdays.

Over pinot noir and small
plates they remember and up-
date. The one on the south side of
the booth is ambivalent about

her sister to the north. She
loves her like a sister, and
like a sister she is jealous of
her apparent success in marriage

and child. The streaked haired
middle sister is depressed
as a reaction to the life crises
she will not reveal. The

birthday girl laughs out
loud and cries inside,
as her son needs rehab.

So the real story is that I
am projecting on to them
my ambivalence and
sadness. I am conscious

of my projections and
they never notice me.

Happy birthday to the dawn
of my consciousness.

Moss

I love the green, tending toward
chartreuse, moss that grows to
decorate the red bricks on the patio.
The moss is Mother Nature's de-

corative touch, to turn the
red squares of baked earth
into art, with a color code
of red and green, stop and

go, in the eye sight of
a common site, my
colorful backyard. A
carpet of spaces transform

squares into verdant life,
evergreen and balanced
creative and revived. I
am observing moss on brick.

Along and Around

Can a walk along and around
the lake be a thread in the whole
tapestry? It may be the whole
tapestry in a thread. Walk.
Talk. Silence. Breath. Movement.
My second son and I worshipped
one Sunday in a walk along and
around the lake. The word was
the talk, the sacrament was the
mysterious presence. Soles
on the path were souls on the
way. It was hot and humid,
our bodies watered in the
summer weather. Body
after soul a slender thread
in the larger tapestry.

To You

This is to you who might
read this word. I need you,
for if a tree falls in the forest
and there is no one to hear it, does
it make a sound? Don't know.

What I do know is if a poem
is written and no one reads it,
it is the sound of silence.
Thank you for reading this word.
You resound the words

as they reverberate through
the space between you and me
and create a transpersonal
invisible sound. Hear me.
This is to you.

Realms

I consistently hear of the
deceased returning to dreamers.
Sometimes, they make a slight
turn of their head, shoulder

high, and walk away. Many
times they appear as cameos,
departing wisdom or assurance.
Occasionally they imply they

are still alive. The frequency
of the appearances appear to
beckon a wonder about this
life and the next. The nexus

of this activity is a central
link between the realms. Time
and space are limited di-
mensions. Die mentions

all dreams where the curtain
between the realms is very,
very thin. Real. What is
real? Realms.

In Heat

That which aligns, connects,
mirrors, fits, and merges
is a "match." Putting human
beings together is "match making."

So why, too, is that phosphorous-
tipped stick, which, with friction,
ignites into a flame called
a match? Striking. Don't we

call a new love a flame?
Isn't fire that which merges and
transforms? When we find
a match, a flame is ignited.

Eros is red, like fire and
is the heat that creates a
match. Like when one is on
fire, having made a match.

We say animals are "in
heat."

See the Tree

Here is how to prepare to die.
Watch a tree, which does it
every year. It appears to
be laborious, painful and barren.

And then . . . rebirth, bud,
bloom, blossom. This is not
a metaphor, simile or analogy.
This is the truth. I have eyed

it with my own insight. Tree-
mendous. Here is how to
prepare to die. Trust the
process. Go with the flow.

See the tree?

Decipere

There are several invitations
about which one must be-

ware. "Have you got a minute?"
"I hate to be the one to tell you."

"It tastes just like chicken."
Watch out! Each invites

deception. That minute
will be an hour. You are

so pleased to be the one to tell
me. If it tastes just like

chicken, why aren't we
eating chicken? Self deception

deceives. Decipere is Latin
for ensnare. Don't get

trapped by a deceptive
invite.

Easter Chicks

One Easter we were given,
by a well-meaning neighbor,
Easter chickens. They were chicks.
One dyed blue, one red, one

left yellow. What temporary
joy. What then to do with
three chicks who would
surely become chickens.

As fate would find us,
my grandfather raised
chickens. So, one week-
end, we made poultry

pilgrimage to take chicks
to the roost. Blue, red,
and even yellow, the chicks
were rejected by the flock.

To be an Easter chicken is not
always popular within the pen.
But with Father Time and Mother
Nature the Easter chicks

lost their artificial personae
and became authentically
chickens. Somewhere in here
is the lesson that Easter

teaches: Be who you are.
Several years later, at Easter,
we went to my grandparents.
For lunch, we had fried

chicken. In some poetic
justice, Granddad thanked
God, for the three Easter
chickens we were about

to eat. Such an Easter
lesson of authenticity
death and rebirth. Or
a simple story of life's

chain and cycle which
is to be found in three Easter
chicks.

How I Got My Totem

In a big dream, a bald
eagle flew from the corner
of my eye into the top

of a giant oak. I was a
shaman, with a stove pipe hat.
I too could fly and joined
the other, bald and bald, tree top high.

Then, a caravan of marauders
rolled by the tree trunk.
I flew in the midst and
was overwhelmed by the mob.

The eagle swooped,
wings spread wide, and
plucked me from my
hubris. Eagles symbolize

power and wisdom. My
inner eagle taught me the
wisdom of power. He

empowered me to learn
not to overpower. This
image I imagine contin-
ually. Courage and wisdom
are the wings of an eagle.

Poet at Play

The writing of a poem
puts the poet at a dis-
advantage. Poetry defies
definition. The poet who
knows what a poem is
is not a poet. In spite of
the dramatic and romantic,
we are conduits. The word
becomes flesh through us.

Now, in order to be a conduit,
one must use study, reading,
listening and faith to be-
come a super conductor
for the word stream that
flows from somewhere
to here and now. The
path to the poem is to
puncture pretense, de-

flate hubris and play.
The poem comes from the
poet at play. Not defining
a poem puts the poet at
an advantage.

The End

Who serves whom? This
is a good question in any
context.

In the Grail Legend, the
question was whom does the
grail serve?

The Fisher King held a chalice
from which he could not
drink.

This created a "wasteland"
and an epic poem by
T. S. Eliot.

Such a good question of
institutions, relationships and
systems.

For the writer, does he
serve the words or do the words
serve him?

Perhaps we should abandon
the servant, hierarchy and
seek equality.

The words serve. That
dot is a period. The writer
serves words.

So no conclusion. What
purpose does that serve?
The End.

Limen

Curious—the Latin word,
"limen," has worked its way
into the contemporary vocabulary
of Psychology. "Subliminal,"

means something is at the
doorway of consciousness.
Limen means, "doorway"
or "threshold." Liminality is

that space between conscious-
ness and unconsciousness.
So our psychic movement is
liminal, moving between

the known and unknown.
What a false formula! That
which we know wasn't once
the unknown. We know more

than we know. Do not
limit the liminal to either
the known or the unknown. Know
what I mean?

Same Glass

A wine glass, mouth down,
stem up, in a circle of
light. So, too, a container.

There is an unfulfilled vacancy
in the vessel upside down.
When rotated the base grounds,

the stem supports and the
container, contains. Nature
cannot abide a vacuum.

Fill the unfulfilled and
the circle of light depends
on the brim. At its peak,

the wine brims over and
with ebb and flow the
container contains less

wine and more light. Within
this view, the glass half
empty is full. Wine or
circle of light, same glass.

Early God Image

My paternal grandfather was
tall and stately: a city clerk.
Three piece suit, blue serge he
wore. Gold pocket watch with
chain fob. They lived on a
hill above the railroad track,
and trestle. On summer visits
he would pull the watch from
his vest pocket, placed in his
palm, looking into hand held
time: "Boys, the train is about
to come." And then, the whistle
and click clack on the train
track. Whizzing by, when
a child, I thought he controlled
the train by watch and fob.

Children are keen observers
and lousy interpreters.

Rise and Fall

From where I sit I can
see the sea. I try to avoid
the waves as tongues licking
the shore. That simile has
lost its smile. So how to
find fresh words to picture
a scene anew? Let us avoid
figures of speech. The waves
are water curled with white
edges that rise and fall. No
matter, there is a metaphor
hidden in there somewhere.
Rise and fall? Edge? From
where I sit, I can see the sea.
My site requires figures of
speech to describe my
sight. Sight and site.
I think I'll take a nap.
Rise and fall!

The Door Is Ajar

When the door is ajar,
means it is open. But
when is the door a jar?
One is open; the other is a
closed container. Pardon me
in my literal symbolic
mind. The door is never
a jar. The open door is
not closed to anyone.

The door is ajar, come
in. The door is a jar,
so it is not open, but
a glass container. What
if one placed a jar in the hinge
of a door? We would be closer
but we would miss the point.
The door is not a jar. Be open
to the door being ajar.

Integrated

There is a shortness of breath.
Is that pathology, psycho-
pathology, or ecstasy?
Heart beat, breath drawn: you
take my breath away . . . my heart
skipped a beat. Body meta-
phor for soulfulness.
It is not how many breaths
we draw, but how many times
our breath is taken away, that
enlivens. So ironic,
that which takes away
gives. Breath drawn,
heart beat, rather than dead
beat and broken heart.
The fact that we use body
metaphors for soulful
experience indicates we are
body/soul, not body and
soul.

Kairos

No present like the time.
Relative. No such thing as
time—an illusion. Created
by humans, in a vain
attempt to order the chaos.

Eternal now. We do not
enter eternity, we are
there, which is everywhere,
there isn't a nowhere. Dizzy.
Disoriented. So create, time

and space to ease the ego's
anxiety about what we don't
know: the unknown. Roll
it over again hoping to
overcome the overwhelming

fear that there is not an
essence or fullness of time:

A Muse to Amuse

Amuse and bemuse both assume
a muse. The Greek Goddess has
got us when she amuses us.
What would life be without

the amusing? Abusing perhaps.
Or at least lacking luster.
The lackluster life is no life but
rather the anti-life. Live

spelled backwards is evil.
No laughing matter, life with
out a muse. So we must
muster the energy to invite

the muse to use us to
bring the laughter and lightness
whereby we can fly like the angels.

Rock and Roll

Last night, my second son and I
took a trip, neither back nor forward,
but within. The conduit was that old
time rock and roll, "the kinda music
just soothes the soul" and Tex/Mex
food, a scruffy bar, simple stage, and
a friend's voice of authenticity. Once
before, my boy and I stood ten feet
from Jagger at a Stones concert. In
the midst of "Beast of Burden," he
leaned in and said, "Dad, this isn't
just about the music!" He taught
me about the invisible church and the
sacred camouflaged in the profane.
A table, music, Divine food, were a
eucharistic reminder that the rock
is rolled away.

Grounded

What's up? Much of our life
time, up was better. Aspire was
a spire pointing toward heaven.
In a three storied universe, hell
was below, earth in the middle
and heaven above—the
direction of our aspiration.
Things began to change
when we were admonished
to, "get down," meaning to,
"get with it." And "it" was
here and now. Whatever "it"
is, it is grounded in the earth,
mindful to be here now,
bringing heaven on earth where
manure is fertilizer and
Mother Earth and Father Time
merge to birth Here and
Now. The "it" we are
to get with is not an IT.

Hammock

The rolled bark of the birch
holds the hammock we
hung this year. Taut
womb holds and contains
giving sense of security.

Then the children wrap and
roll one another, creating
laughter, dizziness, and
a freedom into the
ground of their being.

The old man slowly
slides into the sling
and takes note of the
need for security and
a simpler container.

He then rolls out, re-
born, stands tall and
returns to earth, re-
newed, beneath the
firm trunk and rolled bark.

Circular and Circuits

I'm told nature holds no
straight lines. Mother
Nature in her femininity
is circular and circuitous. Only
artifacts have lines that
are without curves. In
radiology, when the radiologist
sees a straight line, it
is pathology. Point being,
all points to the non-
linear as the process of
progress. Life is not linear,
but a spiral, circumambulating
about a center which is also
circumference. Both the circle
and line are important. But
of the two, we must learn
to live with the non-linear
direction and hold the
hope that the circuitous
leads to the center. Faith
keeps us moving in the dizziness
of freedom.

Nap

The word and experience of
nap is connected to a
brief sleep and the soft or
fuzzy surface on fabric.

The nap is either a
brief eye close or the soft
and brief experience of a
smooth cloth. Children

so get this with their
blankies. The soft nap
of the blanket helps soothe
into the sanctuary of sleep.

Nap leads to nap. Soft and
secure is the maternal
transitional object of the
external mother to the

ability to self soothe
with the smooth nap wrapped
in a womb of cloth mother
at nap time.

Vacant Lot

My hope is that I never
contrive a poem. The
manufactured, fabrication
of a voice, is a forced, un-
amusing sound that re-
verberates a hollow and
vacant lot of words with
out soul. True poetry is
not concerned with form and
function to a fault,
but with authenticity, meaning
and novelty. I am sure
I can't contrive that. I am
not sure of anything,
except that last night I rubbed
my grandson's hair while
he ate ice cream with his
grandmother's chocolate sauce.

Soul Food

There were twelve oysters.
Fried. Batter made a light
brown ball. They were placed
carefully on a white platter.
Chopped mango, purple onion and
chives were sprinkled, dusting
the dozen. A sauce, pink of
catsup and horseradish, was
contained in a silver shot
glass. Presentation is important,
but so is taste. Taste, takes the
tongue to its purpose as though
the tongue has openings whereby
sensuous streams of grace
flow toward soul. Crunch is
sound. Sauce is smell. The
tongue is touch, too. "The senses
are the inlets of the soul,"
says Blake.

By My Own Hand

I still "write" poems. I
do not type. Not my type.
I love the look of letters
and words and that I, not
a machine, manufacture the
words and page. So, what
of the sensuous sense
of the pencil on a page?
Then there is the dance of
my hand and the pencil
with my brain and mind.
The perichoresis is reminiscent
of the integration of mind
and body, seen in a word
on a page, written by a real
hand, whereby nothing becomes
something, by my own hand.

Reading Rumi

I'm sitting at a bar reading
Rumi. He grabs my shirt
tail and pulls me into the
sublime, that subliminal
place where the Divine is
in the wine and word.

He takes me by the hem
of my garment to the
underworld of worldly
questions and eternal answers.
The question is always, "Why?"

The answer is, "Love." Such
a responsible response
is appropriate in a never
and always world. Always,
never fear, "perfect love
casts out all fear." I'm

always, never afraid. Pulled
down into the upward flow
of the subliminal energy
that is everywhere therefore
nowhere, center and
circumference. Reading
Rumi took me nowhere.

Ruminating

I'm reading Rumi again. I can't
be the first to ruminate on
Rumi, such an obvious word
play. He writes abundantly
about wine and drunkenness.
Of course any critic would
see the metaphor, but I am
not critical. I think he is
talking about his love for
the fruit of the vine: Divine.
And for his love, as it were,
for the altered state which
leads to the altar. Ruminating
on Rumi. Ruminating.

Please

I love a free afternoon.
I don't know what true
freedom is, but I do know
when nobody or no thing is

expecting me to arrive.
Play, nap, read, write, oil
the "nothing" to do. Maybe
with nothing to do, I can

be. Free to be. What
a day. One cannot waste
a free day. It is free. The
cost is in spending it to

please another. Please.

Arugula

Arugula is said to be
a salad rocket. There is a
bit of bitterness, which
with a bit of olive oil
becomes a bite of bitter-
sweet, let us say, lettuce.

I like it alone, as well in
a salad. Arugula is arguably
a stand alone dish, but
when put on a veal Milanese
we know what its true
nature is: to compliment

and enhance. Let us
meet, tonight at that place
in the center of the garden,
eat veal, sliced clean and
beheld by a fork full of
arugula. There we will
be beyond the leaf that has
taken us there.

Essence and Totality

Boehme utters the words,
"Whatever the self describes,
describes the self." That dimension
of the psyche holds essence
and totality. Description of the Self
demands that it have a capital S. This
helps distinguish it from
ego. Let us now move from
psychology to poetry. Self
seems synonymous with Soul.
The Soul is simply that part of
a person that is immaterial
and immortal. It is also that
essence that is without def-
inition, cognition and con-
scious knowing. So poetry
is a primary medium for expression
of Soul. Soul is what the body
locates in time and space. The
Self describes this as spatio-
temporality, which poetry takes
us beyond or within. So,
the lightning bug shows the
inner light which we
can't put in a jar.

Overwhelment

There are too many and
too much. This is not
       a judgment.

Twin fears of the infant:
abandonment, overwhelment.
       This is the latter.

Too many, too much. The
culture is currently overwhelmed
       with the current.

Flowing with too much in-
formation, traffic, noise,
       and voice of choice.

This voice seeks silence,
simplicity, serenity, and
       no more voice.

Still be, but be still.

Leave the Shades Up

Rumi says home is
that place, "where we
can walk around without
any clothes on." That plays
so many ways. Both
symbol and poet are
true. Such a truth when
we can see inside and out.

Transparent is sans parent where
there is no one to say, "Shame
on you." Naked truth is freedom
to be you and me. Let's
go home to freedom and
come home to autonomy.
I want to go home. I want to
leave the shades up and not

care who sees me. Seize
the moment, walk the walk, bold
steadfast and unafraid. What
music do you want to give you
the beat to free your soul?
How about, "Walk On The
Wild Side?" "You'll
Never Walk Alone." Come
home with me. Hang
up your hang ups and
walk around. Walk
around. Walk around.

The Grove

The Grove is a bistro
two blocks from my
office. I am a regular.
I take my space and

place at the bar. Gray
stone, white leather bar
stools set the scene.
I would love to say

the Grove is groovy,
but it is an urbane
wine bar. I bring the
invisible grooviness,

because I write poetry
there. That ritual
process makes the se-
cular place sacred

space. At least to me
and I get to decide and
designate the space as a
place where the Transcendent

transcends. The Presence
is present in the crab
cakes and the Chardonnay
and the stone bar on

which the process takes
place. Grove, groovy,
noonday good news.
Sacred space.

Oklahoma

I don't know how Rodgers
and Hammerstein knew.
It opened the year I was
born. It was set in Okla-

homa territory in 1906
outside the town of
Claremore, the home
of my hero, Will Rogers.

The song is a backdrop
of my early life. Even
when I played basket-
ball at Oklahoma State

University, the games
announcer would an-
nounce, "Ladies and gentle-
men, the Varsity," and

all would run out of the
locker room to the crowd
singing, "Oklahoma."
I grew up 60 miles from

Claremore: "grand land."
There was no structure
between my house and
pikes peak, "where the

wind comes right be-
hind the rain." Talk,
hawk circles, sky.
How did those Eastern

guys know? Sitting
in a Manhattan apart-
ment writing about
my landscape,

they had great compen-
satory imaginations
for the contrast be-
tween concrete and
earth, between urbane
and authentic. Not to
judge or to compete,
I am pleased that I

knew Oklahoma and
that they knew to write
it into the collective
consciousness as Okla-

homa, OK. And now
I secretly slide into my
memory and sleep assured,
everything will be OK.

It Will Never Die

It is said that only the
poets read poetry. Poetic
        has become a

metaphor. Things and
beings that have an
        imaginative or

sensitive style are
poetic. Poems are poetic
        even if not read.

Poetry will never dis-
appear, even if never
        read. Like Danny

and the Juniors sang:
"Rock and roll will never
        die. It was

meant to be that way but I
don't know why." So say
        we about poetry.

Interesting

Interesting. Dei means
God. Die means to exit
the realm of time and space.
Maybe in die we meet
Dei. "Imago Dei," means
Image of God. My image
of God imagines that the
Imago Dei transcends
realms. Mysteriously the
energy called Dei is in
Die. This is not a play
on words. This is a con-
viction based on experience.
This is not a sermon, this is
a poem. To die is to
discover the Imago Dei,
to which death is not an
end, but an introduction.
Interesting.

Standing

For most of the game he
stood on his seat with his
hand on my shoulder as
a grounding balance. We
were at the largest crowd
to see a football game in
Texas. My grandson
stood, with his balance
coming from my body.
Granddad. Ball
game. Such a symbol
of the game of life.
Pardon me for this
pedestrian metaphor.
But had you known the
energy of his hand
on my shoulder, you would
have known, as I do,
that it is a grand ground-
ing to have your grand-
son hang on the should-
ders of his granddad.

Yes

Are we mysterious grandeur
or pompous dust? I
know both. I aspire to
experience the mystery
within and out. Make
an infinity sign between
my inner and outer
world and non-world.

Then too, the two. I
live from instinct to
appetite. I am but a
complicated combine of
need to survive and
in deed to find meaning
and purpose. Eat
and sleep. Fornicate

to procreate. Pause
there to know both are
present. Divine is sex,
and new truth of seeking
the sacred in the essence
of another. So now, let me
not belabor the point.
Are we mysterious gran-
deur or pompous dust?

      Yes.

More Than . . .

The kitchen is an alchemical
container. Cook. Heat trans-
forms. Formula for turning
common into uncommon
consumption. Some things
remain raw, but with a
tender touch and tossed to-
gether, a new taste
emerges in the alchemy.

The alchemist knows which
process brings gold, the
goal. Marinade, breading,
seasoning, oil, butter,
under the heat transforms.
Each knows the formula.
Next time, think of the
process of preparation,
and execution as more
than mundane—it
is miraculous.

Realm, Real

The sacred thing about being
with one who is dying is
that you are standing next
to the next. There the light
and energy blend with-
out becoming blurred.

One stands next to the
mystery. There is no fear.
There is a sense that the
soul simply transcends
space at the right time.
Being with another as

they move between the
realms makes the next
realm real.

9-11-16: Untie, Unite

Fifteen years ago, the twins
fell—no, were knocked
down. Surreal: daydream,
nightmare. Trying to re-
member the dismembered.
That night my law school
son called his mother: "I
am coming home for dinner."
Comfort food: meat loaf
and twice-baked potatoes,
ample alcohol. Teilhard
opined, "Whatever [humans] are
capable of, they will do."
Haunting. We build the
towers and knock them
down. Interesting religion
derives from "legare,"
which means to "tie back"
like a big ligament. Any re-
ligion that tears apart
is not serving its purpose.
9/11 or the Crusades, religion's
shadow. Shed the light of
consciousness on that which
into tie back will
continue to untie,
rather than unite.

Gibby

Across from Washington Grade
School, was a grocery, burger bar.

Miss Gibson owned and
ran, such a simple business, as

to not have a name, so it
was called, "Gibby's." On

the grill were onions. The patty
perfect. The buns were toasted

with her buttery touch.
On a saw horse table sat

condiments. Then there were
the chili dogs. Fat franks,

split buns, and a ladle of
chili without beans, an art to

eat and not drip on your school
shirt. Hair net, apron, five

feet of ample body: Gibby.
Her business was nurture,

not profit. I have no
idea about her profit and

loss statements. But I
profited: chili dog, cheese

burger, bag of chips, plenty
of catsup and mustard,

an occasional ice cream
sandwich or Mars bar.

Gimme, Gibby and
I'll live an abundant

life.

Change

I save change. I never liked
having loose coins in my pockets,

so, I have three places I place
the change: a closet jar, a

leather box on my desk, and
a pull-out place for change

in my car. I love homo-
nyms to a fault. All the

above is about change. I
feel differently about Change

than I do about change. I
give my change to my grand-

son. Hear the double play?

Change in attitude, change in
direction, change in the weather

are all experiences I cherish.
No way do I hold change

in an artificial container
unless it is money in the bank.

Nod of Knowing

Out where nothing counted
he was considered a "no count."
Ornery, stubborn, uneducated
wisdom, appealed to the

contemporary cowboys. He
sang, "Why do they call
us cow boys, when we are
bull men?" He caught

the nod of knowing from
the boys trying to begin
to be men. We seek to
be, "masters of [our] fate

and captains of [our] soul,"
to touch our tongues to the
salt of soul and to season
our season with the spice

of life. Out where nothing
counted, this no count,
caught the nod of knowing again
from boys trying to be men.

Creosote

I don't know that I can
describe the smell of

creosote. Creosote.
Don't you love the sound?

Creo-sote. It sounds
better than it smells.

As a twelve year old
boy, it seems that creo-

sote poles were every-
where—phone poles, fence

posts, proper in oil field
supports. Pungent is

the beginning description
of the smell of the oily dark

coating preserving the pole.
Supportive, the former

tree, now narrow wood
needing preservation.

Smell and purpose are
poles apart from the goal

and sound of the coating
put on wood to prevent

disintegration into dust,
for a time.

Cellar

In small country towns
in the fifties, there were,

dug in backyards, storm
cellars. Cellar doors tilted

to fit the round mound.
Pulled open, one would

see no waste of space.
There, shelves on either

side of the cellar. Shelved
there, were jars full of

fruits and vegetables
that were put up.

The floor was packed dirt.
Resting there were benches.

There was a kerosene lantern,
a blanket and a metal

water cooler. On stormy
nights, before weather

reports, safety trumped
claustrophobia. Families,

friends and neighbors
felt an inarticulate fear

bonding. Sometimes sirens
would blow, like the wind,

to warn of a tornado.
Such it was in 1956.

In Drumright, Oklahoma,
the only town in which

I ever grew up, a tornado,
as they say, "hit." Six

people were killed. The
siren blew and the

circular wind tore a
path through our village.

Two blocks from our house
the path destroyed all in

sight. Such was my sixth
grade teacher's house. My

Dad and Mother joined an
amateur first responder

team with other neighbors.
My teacher was spared,

as she heard the siren
and wrapped herself

in a mattress from a day
bed. She had cuts and

bruises, but she lived
to teach again. We dis-

covered no dead, but the
trauma still visits

my memory. That night
when the siren's signal

sent us to the cellar,
we celebrated our de-

liverance from the natural
darkness of Mother Nature.

Blue Heron

Vancouver. Outdoor rest-
aurant. Small boxwood
hedge. Second glass of wine.
Blue heron appears, perched

on the hedgerow, his neck
and head were a question
mark. They are wading birds.
I am blocks from the water.

In dreams, birds tend to be
spirit symbols. In this
day dream, the blue flew
to my side to remind me

of the Presence. Heron
here where neither of us
knew the context.
His presence reminded

me that wherever is every-
where the Presence appears
and disappears in a moment
in time beyond. I saw him.
I saw him. He saw me.

Let It Be

I liked the way the little
girl's curls fell and bounced
about her face. Such a natural,
shall we say, curl. I like
the natural. Nature is the root
of natural. Could we sing,
Nature, is second nature to
me now? When I hear,
natural, all tension drops
from my body and all stress
leaves my psyche. I strive
to hear, it is his nature,
when there I am being
not doing. The girl did
not curl, she just let
it be. And it fell
softly at shoulder and
cheek with a natural
bounce. Rhyme and
rhythm are not limited
to poems. Nature is poetic.
So is a little girl's curl.

Sensational

I am sitting in a restaurant
writing another poem. With-
out too much grandiosity,
I can see they look at me with
great curiosity. Who sits
at the bar and writes into
a leather journal? Why
journal here? I like the
sight and sound to stimulate.
I am an introvert and charge
my batteries with solitude.
So to sense, sight and sound
add smell to complete
my typology. The intuition
will come, but when I am
in my senses, the poem
becomes more sensational.

Ambi-Valent

I am ambivalent about
ambivalence. Two
valences make me
ambi-valent. On the
one hand, each valence
has its own truth. But
the ambivalence creates anx-
iety. On the other hand,
two things can be true
at once which are oppo-
sites. A paradox is not
two doctors. My ego
wants either or. My self
knows either AND or.
Therefore, life would be less
anxious if there was no
ambivalence. But at the
same time life would be
robbed of substance that
is woven into its tapestry.
Gold, silver, red, green,
and black threads are
essential to the depth
of life's tapestry. The
opposite of black and white
is not gray. Gray is the inte-
gration of light and dark,
each retaining its own
integrity.

Nimbus

How can nimbus mean
both halo and dark cloud?
How could it not mean both?

Anyone with a halo also
has a dark cloud. How
can a human hold a

halo without eventually
being hailed low? Such a
tension is in all humans:

angelic and animal;
light and dark; light and
heavy. Such is the predictable

predicament of a human
being, being human. Ah
ha! is the animal and human.

Field Of Dreams

At my grandson's baseball
game, a flock of parakeets
flew through the field. They
somehow parroted the
field of dreams: chatter,
diamond, park. Parakeets
chirping their playful song.
Children playing a pastime,
in time, while the winged-
ones put color in the natural
pallet of Mother Nature.
They were color commentators.

Sensuous

The vacant bedroom at
the light of day is full of
illumination. Natural, as
Mother Nature can't abide

a vacuum. She sheds light
where there was none. She
fills the vacant room with
her fullness. So, OK, now

in the natural sense
of our desire for mother
fulfillment, why can we
not see the light? We

must be more sensuous,
(see the us?) for She fills
all vacuums that long for
Her presence, if we have

the eyes to see. We'll talk
about Father Time another
time.

Simple and Easy

I have learned not to confuse
simple with easy. So many

things that are so simple and
simply so. And yet, to implement

the axiom of simplicity may
be Mt. Everest of easy. Let it go.

So simple, but how do you
let it go when you don't have it—

it has you? Turn it off. Simple?
Yes, unless the volume has

no button for control. Not
so easy. Get over it! Fine

in terms of simplicity. But
what if we can only jump so high?

This reflection is an empathic
attempt to empower you to

not confuse simple with
easy. Simple? Easy?

There Aren't Many Adults

I believe it to be healthy
for a child to have an
imaginary friend. I be-
lieve it to be healthy for

an adult to have an im-
aginary friend. That image,
when conscious, creates an
inner companion. Unlike

the child, the adult listens
for the wisdom, truth, com-
passion of the inner one.

Who is to say? Maybe
the child knows, at some
level, that the imaginary
friend is bringing a message

of truth and authenticity
that the fragile ego can't
hold. There aren't many
adults.

Frequent

How frequent is frequent?
If nothing is free, how
about free-quent? Here
I go again. Is quent—Quint?

How about frequent—as being
quintessential? There are
four essences: wind, earth,
fire and water. We are always

looking for the quintessential—
the fifth. How frequently
we/I drift from quent to
quint. But, I can't quit.

Quent, quint, quit. I know
a Quinton who frequently
can't quit. But Quinton
isn't a quitter, nor is he

quiet. Quint, frequently, is
quintessentially my grand-
son. His love is free-quent.

Wait, Weight

I'm still fascinated by words.
What about wait and
weight? Heavy. Light
weight is a person of little

substance. Wait, is such true?
Does a person of heavy weight
have more substance than a
light weight? Must be

that weight is heavy
when talking of substance
and light when talking
of one's weight—though

a light weight can be a
heavy weight. Need I go
on? Thank you. You can
wait for more wisdom.

Tip Top

Once, in the newspaper,
on Saturday's church page,
where preachers listed their
sermon titles, I read my

favorite of all time: "Ten top
tips, for tip top Christians."
Think about it. A tip is
a small point. I suppose

his point was small like
the tip of an iceberg. How
trivial to point to the
tip, when the substance

is under the water. Oh
well. A well is a deep
source of water, makes
one wonder how "well"

also means whole. Super-
can be potent or ficial.
Just a tip, a look in-
side. The tip of a top

ten Christian.

Dizziness of Freedom

I suppose I'm not the
first person/poet to
word play with amaze
and a maze. They both

speak of overwhelment. One
can enter a maze, get
lost and not find a way
out. Amazing! Maze

and craze are cousins
of the grandparents of awe
and awesome. Amaze
plays both ways. Lost in-

deed and awash with
ecstasy, chanting enchant-
ment. Ecstasy means out
side the stasis, the

stability of the stable,
enable one to move past
the past into the novelty
of natural, unknown

para-normal, into the
cloud of unknowing. My
pen echoes my mind in
the dizziness of freedom.

Carlsbad Caverns

In the 50s we would
travel in un-airconditioned
cars. The open windows were
sustained winds and cut
off communication.
My brother and I
chose to substitute fighting
for intimacy. Dad would
stop the car and threaten
us if we didn't stop.
Read. Sleep. Count car
licenses. Travel was
abusive, expensive
and seldom. We went
from Oklahoma to
Carlsbad Caverns, New
Mexico. Was it worth
the abuse and expense?
I still remember and
write a poem about the
awesome trip to see
the incredible natural
cave. It is our nature
to travel to the awesome—
cost what it may.

Peas If You Please

I don't know the difference
between a restaurant and

a diner. Since this place
is called "24/7" and has a

bar and vinyl booths, I
presume it is a diner.

It has on the menu,
under "Sides," purple hull

peas. My grandmother
and mother would

put a pile of peas
on a newspaper and

we would shell
the peas. Somewhere

between task and ritual,
the purple hulls would pile

on the daily newspaper
and pardon the pedestrian

rhyme: the peas would
please. At the 24/7 diner

they qualify for local
and organic fare. I

am dining at a 21st
Century diner. Farm

to table defying the
tradition of frying.

Sitting still for a
salad of Village Farms

Tomatoes, Pedernales
Farm arugula and

J. B. Farms bi-colored
sweet corn. Tonight

I will go to a cafe
and order fried chicken,

fried okra and corn-
bread. Life is varied and

compensatory. I actually
prefer the peas, if you please.

Source Once Resource

I want to thank that Source
that provided colors. Especially
the delicate shades. More

specifically the shades of
green in the trees. Isn't it
interesting that trees have

shades and provide shade?
No, I mean it—I find such
meaning in the sense of

indigo, one of the seven
in the rainbow. Purple?
Blue? Yes. Shade is the

subtle blend. I love the
paradox of a subtle blend
being bright: orange,

red and yellow. I will
never take for granted the
sensation we are given in the five.

Sight, sound, taste, touch, smell
are gifts of the Source that gave
us color. I was, this morning,

looking at the trees and marveling
at how the subtle shades of green
get their depth from the sun

light. Thank you, Source. What
a resource, for experiencing
the presence of you in color.

OK, So

OK, So, What a beginning.
OK, So, This is all there is?
OK, So, You know?
OK, So, What's next?
OK, So, Tell me the truth.
OK, So, Why now?
OK, So, Why you?
OK, So, This means?
OK, So, Why us?
OK, So, Help me?
OK, So, Get over it!
OK, So, What does this want?
OK, So, We are on our own.
OK, So, What is the solution?
OK, So, Let it go!
OK, So, How?
OK, So, I don't know.
OK, So, I get it!
OK, So, It is over?
OK, So, It begins.

Legacy

Today I edited. To pour
through the poems, to
re-break the line, to change
the image, to hear the
phrase weeks later, is
to hear it again for the
first time. Part of the
pleasure of writing poems
is to edit them. Roll it over
like the water polishes the
rock: "pour over it." Like
with one's children, eventually
one has to let them go.
We do not aspire for perfect
children, so it is with a
poem. Birth it, nurture it
and eventually, let it
go. Being a single parent
makes it more imperative
to send the poems into
the world, knowing, being
a perfect parent is the
worst legacy you can
leave.

Complementarity

The quantum physicists
speak of complementarity.
Whereas, it may take an
opposite or another to

complete, there may be
a necessary complement
that is unknown or unseen.
What you see is NOT what

you get. They write about
particle and wave in-
forming, that if one sees the
particle, one cannot see

the wave. And so is such
with the wave. Implica-
tions? There are elements
present that we cannot see

that effect our affect.
In other words, there is an
aspect to the psyche that

is unconscious. There is
also a presence that we
cannot see, but is a
complementarity to our

wholeness. Such can
be seen, but not with
the eyes. In physics,
psychology and spirituality

there is agreement that
there is more than meets

the eye. There is much
more than meets the eye.

Maw

So now, I bury my mother-
in-law. She always referred

to me as her "son-in-love."
Maw, she was. In an ety-

mological rehearsal we are re-
minded that "maw" originally

meant stomach. With an
etymological swallow it

is clear that "maw" is the one
who fills the stomach,

one who feeds and nurtures
like Mother Nature.

My mother-in-love for fifty
plus years fed me, first

as an adolescent boy, then as a man
with children as a GRAND mother.

She acknowledged my work and
when absent, present with

her fulfilling love.
She fulfilled her arche-

typal role as maw, the
one who satiates one's hunger

for food or a symbol of love.
The last words she spoke, as

I did her last rites and
the final blessing of a

kiss, she asked my sister
-in-love, "Has he had

lunch?" Maw, my other
mother, Maw's last words

to me were a lifetime of
fulfillment. Maw.

Compete, Defeat

People pay money to watch
people hit each other. I
see on T.V. adds for shows
where people hit and kick.

I guess I can analyze why
people get a kick out of such.
We still have a reptilian brain.
The stem is territorial, compete

and defeat for victory of terr-
itory. To watch such must
stimulate our animalhood.
Who am I to judge? All I know

is the control is in my hands to
change the channel to some-
thing that educates, inspires
or entertains in a creative way.

I may not get a kick out of it,
but I do rise above the
animal me, at least until
I must find a way to survive.

Time Was

My uncle used to begin
his living in the past by
saying, "Time was . . ."
Time was when a man

could make a deal on a
hand shake. Time was
when a man's word was
all he had.

Time was when children
knew their place. Time
was, when time was. We
may be in a time was.

Now, there is no time. No
future, no past. The
circle on your wrist is
gone time was. Essence,

fullness of time. In the
future which isn't we
won't say, "Time was."
Just, time is.

Reel And Real

I read today a poem in
which the poet wrote,
"the stars reel." My homo-
nym mind played with
reel and real. When I
fish, "I reel 'em in."
When I let my mind reel,
I wonder—what is real?
Spinning, reality is the
conscious altering of con-
sciousness. Really? Reeling
in fishing is real. And
in the stars? What is real?
Reeling stars causes the
mind to reel about what
is real. This is really where
I always end up with my
mind really reeling. Oh
my!

Nature's Palette

I haven't studied the birds,
flowers, and the other parts
of Mother Nature's palette.
I think of them as art. Each bloom
and blossom is art. Some-
times my grandson will explain
the birds and trees. He is a budding
scientist. For me, my eyes
frame the landscape with
tree, flower, bird and sky
like the original painter put
it there, everywhere. Humans
many times block my view with
buildings and human made
barriers to blind me to
the natural art from the
original artist, who with
her divine palette,
brush and paint, draws
the perfect painting with
all its imperfections.

Fire and Wine

What would Rumi do with-
out fire and wine? Most
of the time I have known
him, he was either drunk

or aflame—no difference
between the two. One from
love, the other from the
beloved. Both from the

same source. Both re-
source for the human trans-
cendent movement to the
divine moment for which we all

live. For fire and wine,
one transforms, the other in-
forms of transcendent energy
like a flame can inflame

and alter consciousness
as the fruit of the vine
is divine. "Turn this
wood to fire."

Alone Together

I am in a public
place. Pub derives from
public. So it is OK that
the guy next to me keeps

glancing one eye toward me
writing this poem. He wonders
what I am writing and so do
I. If he knew I was writing

about him, he would wonder,
as I do, what am I saying?
Who wears a black T-shirt
with a black coat? Who has

a 3 to 5 day beard? Who
stares ahead through a glass
of white wine? Who uses
his phone like a companion?

He is we. Alone seeking
connection. He stays
on his phone. And I write
this poem.

Quiet Shaking Limbs

Cold, rainy nights are poems
of experience. The next day's
reflections attempt to inte-
grate the experience of the
sound of rain peppering a
tin roof and the temperature
creating a shiver 'til the
cover quilt and smooth
sheet, pulled chin tight,
can capture body heat and
quiet the shaking limbs.

No word can re-create the
mellow taste of Weller
bourbon, but it can
re-mind the experience.
And with a bit of imag-
ination create a new
experience. Thank God
for memory and imagination.
Rain on roof, slight shiver,
and then the memory of a
mellow Weller. Sublime.

Timorous

So now the calendar reels
toward pregnancy. It is
not as if we don't know
what is coming. And

yet, that has never come
this year. A new, Advent.
This timorous season is so
because of the fear of what

might happen if the In-
carnation, incarnates. Now
we have unpacked the symbol
into a fact. God is in

the world, more importantly,
my world. So much
responsibility. What is
an appropriate response?

Not for me to say. My role
is to remind of the response:
sentimentalize, idealize,
deny or project onto another.

If the holy, divine, sacred,
transcendent, numinous Pre-
sence manifests in my
ordinary life, what will

be my responsibility?
You must decide. For me
I will look in every corner
of the world for the faint

sense of the Presence. And
breathe it into my life and
into those I love. They
don't need to know.

But, if they do, we will
have a merry Christmas.
A particularly meaningful wisp
of incarnational energy.

Narrow Ridge

How do you know to do this?
You know, live your life in
relationship and ultimately
alone. She/he can compan-
ion, but not complete. Every
relationship is incomplete,
as no other can complete.

Cynical? Healthy?
Tell me of your experience.
If they (he/she) are to
complete, what is your ex-
perience? How do you
know to do this? Hold the
one in your right hand

and the other in your left.
He/she cannot complete
me, but he/she can walk
the narrow ridge side by
side holding hands and
helping when one falls
off the narrow ridge.

Well Being

I am rewarded for writing
poems. The reward is not
monetary, but is found in
the brain chemistry which

sends signals to the mind
that there is a well being.
This being flows through
the images, symbols, poetic
pictures of landscape and in-
scape, inescapably revealing
the infinity symbol running
from outer world to inner

world. The reward of the poem
is the realization that inner
and outer are one. The brain
secretes secrets that soothe
in alliteration, the being,
with well being.

At Home

When we lived in Herrods
Creek, we cut our tree. The
boys were boys and Allison
was the sheepdog. We piled
into the Suburban station
wagon, pretending to be a
real wagon, off to the
country six miles away
to find the perfect tree.
Only to be reminded, in
nature there is no perfection.
So we took the borrowed

chain saw, pretending
to be an axe, and cut
a tree that leaned a bit to
the left and was ten inches
too tall. Bungee cords were
rope, and atop of the
wagon we tied the perfect
tree. At home, the maternal
had prepared place and decor-
ations for the bent, too-tall,
perfect tree. Gene Autry
sang, corn popped, and

though we had no "chest-
nuts roasting on an open
fire," we did have "Jack Frost
nipping." The fire-warmed
night was truly warmed with
love of people for one another
and their sons and an English
sheepdog and the sentiment
of an evening that will

disappear in time, but
remain present in memory.
That night, we were safe,
warm, fed, and at home.
Thanks for the memories.

Nature Is Natural

This time of year the pecans
fall. Squirrels gather. And
dropping on a standing seam
steel roof at five A.M. in the
morning delivers an irritating
interruption and a warm sense
of nature's cycle. When I arise
with sleep in my eye, I see the
doves feasting on the nutty night
of nature's residue in my
drive. It is all played
out in nature and
human nature. The interrup-
tions and untimely events are just
right for the bigger picture
than my comfort. She
wins, though there is no
competition. I do not lose.
Nature is natural, even
on a standing seam steel
roof where squirrels harvest
and drop pecans awakening
me into a secure sense
of being nurtured by the
natural, while muttering
"Nuts!"

You Know

Not often do I feel at a loss
for words. Even if I did,
I would express it. Such
doesn't always mean that the
words have meaning, but
the words are meant to have
wings, to fly to the nest
of hope, incarnation, resur-
rection. You know, you know.
Sometimes, I have no words;
that is when I say: "You know."
You know? "In the beginning
there was the word."

Slight Curl

So, I sat with a man today
whose life of circumstance
and coincidence had brought
him to a dark place. Loss,
rejection, humiliation
had put him in the complex-
ity of a psychic complex. Aban-
doned, overwhelmed, he
cried for the power to
sit with the affect rather
than to end the pain. The
only power I had to empower
him was empathy. We
sat. I told him I couldn't
get him out of his hole,
but I could sit with
him in it 'til we could
find his way out. We
sat still. He committed
to the hero's greatest
quality: perseverance.
He reflected that he felt
abandoned. I promised
him that I would not
abandon him if he would
promise not to abandon
himself. His lips had a
slight curl.

Mark 9: Salt and Fire

Salt and fire. "For everyone
shall be salted with fire."

So Jesus' enigma was his
style—not to confuse so

much as to enlighten.
Fire consumes and trans-

forms; salt preserves
and enhances. So it is.

His words are salt and fire,
paradox, ambivalence, am-

biguous, can confuse or
clarify. One must dig

deeper than simple reason
to comprehend the un-

reasonable. Such con-
sciousness is birth:

Pain and labor. So
we ignore or dis-

tract. No bumper
sticker reads: "Honk

if you love ambiguity!"
"Salt and fire" is a mean

saying, meaning, whatever
it means to you. Be

authorized to be your
own authority.

Dead Doves

Sauntering to lunch today,
on the side walk

I saw two dead doves. Being
intuitive, I wondered

what was the meaning? Two
dead doves. Doves

are spirit symbols. The Holy
Spirit is a descending

dove. It is the week before
Christmas Spirit dead?

Death in dreams means transforma-
tion. What is being trans-

formed? What being is transformed?
Sure, sometimes a

dead dove is a dead dove—
but two? When

I get an "Ah Ha," I'll
get back to you.

My last thought is that they
symbolize a new

beginning. Ah Ha!
We also live in a

world governed by natural
laws. Two things

can be true at once.
Two dead doves

symbolizing new life?

Wine Quiets the Whine

One more and a check. That
code signals no more after
one more. The ritual is to
have two glasses of wine at
lunch on a day when I
can take a nap. Rare day
is a holiday from respon-
sibility—that day when the
grape quiets the grip of the
complex, complex which has
a voice of one's worth is
in one's work. Wine quiets
the whine. One more and
a check. No. Just one
more. Just one more and
maybe. Maybe.

I Love You, Jack

I just wrote a note to my friend
Jack who has had metastatic
cancer. We were runners.
We ran every Sunday for decades.

He is funny, not as funny as
he thinks, but funny enough.
He laughs at his own jokes
and slaps you on the back

when he thinks he has said
something truly funny. We
both know the back slap is
our affectionate touch for

males who love one another.
How can we express the
love of men for men? So
afraid of homosexuality.

Never fear. What we should
fear is not expressing our
love for one another. So
this poem. I love you, Jack!

Pileated

I like the sound of a
woodpecker—heard one

today. Such a sound took
me to another: pileated.

How appropriate. Perched
claw deep in the birch bark

is a pileated woodpecker.

Could be a bird with a big beak,
but no, it is, as I have said,

"Pileated." *Rat a tat tat,*

beak against birch bark.
Leaves leave shadows

swaying like lace on
the green summer lawn.

And the pecking is from
a pileated winged one.

Sole/Soul

She said she wanted my
soles to be cumfy—such
a multi-layered gift from

my granddaughter. House
shoes that had firm soles
to go outside when called.

Cumfy was the word she
used in the secret Santa
note with my comfortable

new inside/out shoes.
She was not conscious that
soles, the foot's bottom,

is where the Soul enters the
body, as it could never enter
through the head. Clementine

gave me a gift to firm
my Soul and to protect
it from any harsh surface.

Cumfy. Soul food
granddaughter. Maybe she
did, at some level, know

her gift protected my Soul.
I know her hair and
smile are Soul food.

Still Born

I heard a dream today that
Christ is a stillborn baby.
The dreamer felt confused and
a bit sad that the Christ child
was still born.

Then she realized the dream
maker had put the message
in an ironic homonym.
Christ is not born without life.

But this year, the Christ is
still born again. But, may
be she must breathe the soul
into the baby to animate him.

All this new myth was to
take place in her. The Christ
is still born in her
psychic barn. Now needing

her to animate him.

Sentimentality

Sentimentality seems to be
a sentinel against taking
responsibility for the opposite—
for the dark, the painful, the
brutal. But such a one-sided
attitude when pushed to its
extreme becomes its
opposite. We have a sweet
Jesus, prince of peace, god of
love that we want you
to love. And if you don't
accept him, we will kill
you. Thus the sentimentality
of the Crusades.

Rainbow Reigns

The light through the paned
glass, refracts through my wine
glass to create a rainbow
on my poet's page. When
I write the bow dances in a
moment in time, beyond time.

Why does this sign of the
covenant bow before me?
Bow. Bow. A rainbow bows.
A bow is a knot that ties two
things together. A stringed
instrument is a bow. So now

I know, a bow bows be-
fore me making a bow of
two strings that knot
to make a sound of a
banquet gathered at
wineglass, bending light

into a rainbow reigns.
Bow. Wow!

"A Hell Of a Man"

I heard Terry Allen again
last night. First heard
him near forty years ago.
We were in Tyler and Lubbock

was on everything. Four de-
cades down the highway,
everything is still there.
The Amarillo Highway is

still a "hard ass." The
"Great Joe Bob," is still bad.
How about the "vinyl tuck-
and-roll?" She still sits
"naked in that chair that
came from France." I can
smell the "truckload of
art, even though I weren't

around." "The cracker still
crunched," and we rode
anew that "New Delhi Freight
Train." "My ego ain't my

amigo" anymore, as we await
"Pink and black to come
back." Saw Jo Harvey,
still waltzing, and
laughed at Mavis and

her snapping turtle spine.
40 years later you are
just as animated, still
smiling, raunchy, shoulder

pitched. You are the same
except more so. Transcendent,
immanent, human, and
a hell of a man.

I Missed Him

Today is my brother's 76th birth
day, though he didn't live to
see it. Such memories of him
make me hit the paradox of progression
and regression. I pray for the
reconciliation of the next
realm and re-member intricate
details of our early life. He
was my protector and provocateur.

He would always protect me
from all external enemies
except him, who thought I
was an incompetent idiot.
In all fairness his older sibling
attitude toward me was
natural. Some of it honed me
to face the world with
lack of fear, and some of

his critique was damaging.
I have long ago forgiven him for
his natural abuse, but all psycho-
dynamics aside, what I would
like most this day would be
a brotherly hug and a warm
rehearsal of the good memories
which would heal the negative.
Such healing would turn the
negative memories into healing
and wholeness. Today is my
brother's 76th birthday. I miss
him. I missed him.

Their Hair

So natural: Hair. How
human to seek beauty
in how one fixes one's
hair. I speak of female,
though not exclusively.

For many their hair is
their organizing principle.
In fact we find ways to
adorn with beauty our
natural traits. Hair on our

heads is to protect from
the bad rays and to
warm. But to seek beauty
in wave, curl, color, bun,
tail and twist, is human creativity. I like

humans who take the natural
and comb beauty into mundane
growth. I sit in a rest-
aurant of many tables. At
each, people chat beneath

hairdos—styled
parted, curled, colored and
combed. Just a reflection on the
human need to create
an heir to creativity
in their hair.

Flow/Flower

Time to write again. Let it flow
like water falling down the rocky
ridge. More so like lava erupting
from the underworld of the volcano.

More like tears at the birth of your
first grandchild. Flow: to roll
down, to stream, to fall down.
All attempt, in this piece to des-

cribe how words come out
to flow into flower. When
it is time to write again,
do not capture the words, but

let them flow. Let them flow.
Flowers.

When Time Was Born

For Grace and Travis

When time was born from
the womb of nowhere, these
two would dance their path
to meet here at this moment.
Here for a monumental vow to
define love for one another.

The world waits with held
breath, to hear the vow worded,
the hands joined, the rings,
circles of gold, signifying
wholeness, exchanged to
change the commitment to a covenant.

The two merge in order to
emerge into a sum of
partners greater than the
whole. Today the top of
the time space box is
blossoming in order to enter
eternity. This mysterious
moment is the essence of the presence
and fullness of time—never
before and never again.
The two become one and
the one empowers the two. What
happens in this Kairos is
incomprehensible in Chronos,
but known as ensouled
where, soul mates dine
on soul food, mana from
heaven: the sacrament of
Holy Matrimony.

I Need to Write a Poem

You know, to scratch the
itch; to ease the pain, to be
placed in the present; to serve
the purpose . . .

So, as to not contrive, I'll
picture my grandchildren
playing in my front yard.
Here is a photograph:

Each blonde beneath a
blue sky with lamb-like
clouds. They laugh and
scream like the birds

flying, tree to tree. Now,
it is a whiffle ball,
next will be tag, then
badminton with a unique

shuttlecock and new racquets.

I sit in my lawn chair
not as potentate, but
as photographer. Picture
this: itch scratched, pain

palliated. Presence present.
Purpose served. I needed
to wrote this poem, or
maybe it wrote itself.

Moist Eye

I saw my son lecture. How
can I report my thoughts and
feelings? He was articulate, present,
funny, informative, authentic.

This not about me but about
my reaction. Brain chemistry:
rush of the chemicals that gift
a sense of well being. Of

course pride, but more so a
sense of humility, conn-
ected to the whole. Seeing
him serving his purpose gave

my life a purposeful presence
of having contributed some-
thing greater than myself
through which I found my-

self in giving him to the
world, not as a reflection
of me, but as a reflection
of him in my moist eye.

Graceful Time

Friday afternoon without
any appointments is a
dangerous time. Why not slip
away and sip a bit of wine
in order to initiate a nap?

So where is the danger? Must
be in the inner voice of an
anachronistic father complex:
Lazy, nonproductive, irr-
esponsible. But after

a bit of the vine the voice
changes to healthy, self care,
spiritual the nap is a
map home, to the place we
long to belong, the under world

beyond time and space
within spactiotemporality
and without prohibition.
Friday afternoon without app-
ointments is a graceful time.

Minding the Mind

There was just this little
time to wander and contemplate
the mindlessness of mind-
fulness. I can't get my

mind out of the way. So I
say, "never mind." So now
I quiet the mind, to mend
the stress and remind my

self of the need to contem-
plate the presence which
offers the "peace which passeth
all understanding." I am

re-minded of the possibility
of peace, the probability of
centering the off center sense
of unbalance, integrated into

the whole. Wholesome, Holy,
Wholly, a small time, beyond
time, timely to contemplate
getting my mind around:
                    mindfulness.

Sacred and Profane

Alone with pen and pad. No one
watching. No one monitoring the
movement from sacred to profane.
No one to differentiate, the
difference, as if there is one.
There is one difference between
the sacred and the profane, and
that is that one is the other re-
versed. I don't know the difference
until one points out the difference
then be assured there is no
difference. Sex. Making love.
                    Amen.

Dynamic

Where to begin? I suppose
one doesn't just begin. Each
has a before we began. That
fare that was begun before.

So what sense to make of this
being that always had a
before? We do not end a
phase of being, we accumulate.

We are all we have ever been
and can regress to any previous
phase. I am two and four-
teen. So when I begin, I

bring all before to the fore
and confront that which
is in front of me, never
knowing when to begin

or when to end. The end
of the beginning is the be-
ginning without end.
The end. Begin again.

Bubble Nugget

He told me his rap name
was Bubble/Nugget. Transparent,
effervescent, vivacious, winsome.
Nugget: a solid lump of
gold, unique, stable, valuable.

So the dynamic, solid,
transparent lump of gold
came to me last night after
a day of swimming, play,
games, chasing and fighting

with his brother. It was late.
He took his blue blanket,
worn like a stole, and
snuggled in against me.
A transparent lump of

gold, he fell asleep under
my wing, wrapped in
his rap name: Bubble/
Nugget. A lump of gold,
bubbled down under my side.

After the Fall

So, I had a leg thing.
I fell on my hardwood
stairs and the stair
edge, cut and bruised my
skin. In classic
long range denial, I let
it go. Until today
when the swelling, red
and blue wound asked
me to see a healer.

Low and behold, the
wound wound up being
in the healing process.
In spite of its appearance a
metaphor for Psyche
and soul, or sign of
significance of the
progress of a process of
making whole includes a
wound and scar: a
sign of healing.

The Center We Seek

I am sure that I am not
sure of much. Surely,
that is the honest summation
of the human predicament.

Unpredictable, the human
path. Labyrinth like,
with twist and turn and
dead end and new beginning.

We take our turn toward
our end. In a maze one
can get lost and never return.
But, with a labyrinth, if one

keeps moving, amazingly,
one will arrive at the center
of one's quest. The center
is the home we so seek.

Keep moving circuitous in
a circumambulation is the circuit
that connects with the whole.
Whole is the center we seek.

Now and Never

Finn is eleven. How can that
be? Being is becoming. Finn, at
one time a little being, is
now taking his place in be-
coming. A grand grand-
son he is. Appropriately
and naturally, all is about
him. And at the same time
he honors how his family
has formed and informed him
of who he is in the world and
the nature of the world he is
in. Some accurate, some
not. Only he can discover
and discern what is his
truth vs "the truth," if such so
exists. For now, he smiles,
rebels, connects, regresses,
and progresses. Eleven is
the second decade. Welcome
to the next phase. Teach me
to be eleven again, and I will
meet you where we are the same
and never again.

What?

What? The best question.
Where all does it lead thee?
What? So what? means
both what does this mean and
what does this not mean? So
now we are back to the mean
time: mean in between;
mean = average. Mean
not civil. What is the
mean time. What is the right
question. Or is it a state-
ment? What may be the
only question. What?
What, may lead one to the
one truth. What is truth?

So sorry so very
sorry!

Imago Dei

I revel in the sound of Imago
Dei. M ago Day ee. Why
not? M ago DAY ee.
God, you know deity. Remember
God created humans in his
own image. Remember how
that which is dismembered
is remembered in the Imago
Dei. Day ee. M ago. Long
ago the mago was created and is
still, though not still, is moving
in a dynamic movement to
the essence. M ago moves
to the center and essence of
who we are. Created as creatures
by the creator as Images of
him/her self, whatever
Dei means, it is meaningful.
Day ee, Dei each day means the
expectation of essence. Essentially
the Imago Dei is central to the
sound of the revelatory experience of
the sound meaning of Imago
Dei.

September 22

Today is the day I was born.
Born to bear the gift and

burden of the birth I did
not request, to the grave I

cannot escape. Life
is to be home, in the

lightness of being. Born.
Borne. Life is the spectrum

between the polarities; the
two opposites which are one.

Born, borne, joy and
sorrow, ecstasy and

agony. Born to be-
come me. That which

is never before and never
again. No other, not another

has this task of bearing
my being. So, my particular
purpose is to honor that instant

where this instance entered
lusting to find a life and

give it away. I watched
a daylily make a trumpet

and leave. I saw her
beauty, heard her hum,

and watched her petals
fall. Today is the day

I was born to bear life.
The petals are the polarity:

born to fall. Bearing
beauty. Born to bear,

life is to be borne and
reborn.

Day Dream

The poem may be considered a
day dream. Symbol and image
are in both. Both are involuntary
and carry something of the un-

conscious. The dream maker
is the same, whether by day
or not. The poem is the day
dream of the poet. If he

gets out of the way the
pen opines in a way
of its own. Ownership
is irrelevant. The truth

is sought in the language
of the poem. Do not
analyze or interpret.
Let the dream be an

experience by day, by
day dream. So now we know
less, more so, about the poetic
process as day dream.

Face the Day

This is that day when
day time narrows.
The profile of the
day's face becomes

more definitive. The brows
arch, the nose points,
the lips pout, the chin
tucks firmly into the

neck. Let's face it—
the day has a beauty
like that of forehead to chin.
Name the day for its

countenance, behold
the day, as a daydream.
And kiss its pouted
lips. Face the day.

Life Is Possibility

Possibility—perhaps this is the
definition of life. Pretense
is the denial of possibility for
it decides, controls, and presumes
the illusion that all have any
control. Pretense and pretend
are mother and child. Pretense
is an attempt to make something
that is not the case appear true.
Of course we seek certainty

to assuage our anxiety
about the uncertain. When we
frame life as possibility,
anything is possible.
For the paltry ego whose
world view is small, meager,
petty, and afraid, un-
certainty is full of fear.
Possibility for the mature
ego, makes the impossible

possible; the novel, never
before, and the unknown
known. Life is possibility,
not predetermined by fear
or fantasy. Be open to the
possibility, that is life.

Glazier and Joiner

I was sitting in a chair
near the window. The pane
frame was wooden. The
glass would have been be-
velled, but for the necessity
of putting the pane in a frame.
The glazier was not so much
an artist as a pragmatist.

I respect the glazier's gaze,
knowing the goal was to
bring light into the room by
the means of molded wood,
good glass and a fine frame.
I was sitting in a chair near
the window. The joiner who
made the chair was also there.

Chill Out

First day of Autumn chill,
I wonder what the animals
feel? They know better than
we, that the biorhythm
seasons, seasons. Now is
the time when the body has
a mind of its own. One
rubs hands together to
symbolically warm, but
to bring heat to chilly
hands. Do the rabbits be-
gin their leap home? Do
the armadillo care? All
I know is today I found a
bounce in my step like the

rabbit hop seeking shelter
and the warm, warmth
of body and soul, the
dimension of Psyche that
sees the fall as a time of gray
from the solar certainty of
a summer sun. Now
all move to the Mother Season
where she wraps her arms
around our fresh feeling
of cool which changes our
body/soul in a simple
change of seasons, where the
cool air against our cheek
heralds that change is

necessary and healthy.
Such wisdom comes
from the first day of
Autumn chill: naturally,

color bends, breath slows,
body slacks, and we fall
into the change that the
first Autumn chill calls
to us. Respond. Respond
in a passive way that
accepts the fullfill-
ment of the seasonal
statement of the Autumn chill.

Lying

I must imagine your presence,
and cadence of your breath, lying
next to me. You see, you are
not next to me. Isn't cadence

or rhythm, you know, the sys-
tematic arrangement of sounds?
This is the poet's problem. Even
in imagining you beside me in

bed, I am distracted, trying to
find the right word for my
imagination to use to describe
your breath. Even though you are

absent, I want to bring you be-
side me, by my imagination.
Second best, unless one makes a
poem of your presence, in your absence.

Which is real—the memory and
imagination or your absence when
you are present? Lie beside me
and let's talk. I imagine you

asleep in our attempt and
your breath is a beat, cycle
recurring at regular intervals
syncopated sounds of your

lying: beside me.

Solace

I'm learning to live without
solace. So much of life is
question, especially around trauma,
pain, accident, illness, for
which we naturally seek solace.

But I speak not of just
injustice. What of the great
questions? What of the human
predicament? Here we are torn
between a birth we did not

request and a grave we
cannot escape, seeking solace
for the anxiety of not knowing.
We fear non-being and seek
solutions which we believe will

bring solace. I am learning
to live without solace. Last
night my grandson snuggled
in against my side and sought
solace in his grandfather. He

slipped into a peaceful sleep.
I took great solace in his
warm body, rhythmic breath,
and innocent surrender
to the solace of sleep.

Labyrinth

Have you ever walked a
labyrinth? If you haven't
do not read on. If you are
intrigued, go walk one,
and return to this circuit-
ous, poetic circumambulation.

One of this one's favorite analogies
for life's journey is the
labyrinth. The essence, distilled
from waterfalls of words, is
the movement, the journal of
the journey. In the journey of

the labyrinth, if you just
keep moving you will reach
the destination, the center, the
home, the goal. There are U-
turns, distances, twists and turns,
but just keep moving and you

reach the center. In a maze
you can get lost and never
emerge. In the labyrinth if
you persevere, the goal will be
met, found, discovered, arrived.
I shall not seek another synonym.

What you must now know and feel
is that the labyrinth is metaphor and
analogy for the journey
toward wholeness.
Read this poem and keep
walking.

Flannery and the Beach Boys

Having just read from Flannery
O'Connor's journal, I feel less
ambivalent about my ambivalence.
Her world view views the world
in a non-sentimental sentiment,
seeking the transient in the
incidental. She has informed
me in a formative way about
non-sentimental religion. Ugly
might be beautiful. Resonance
is that which sounds meaningful,
that which vibrates good vibra-
tions. Flannery resonates. I
am this day in an ironic
sound from another day and
sounds, picking up good vibrations.

Morning Glory

For Gretchen and Trey

My quotidian word trek
was today awakened by
a climb of morning glories.
On a pole at the corner of
no and not, I saw a resounding
yes! There they were, climbing
in their lavender/purple glory.
In no surprise, they grew
up from pole to wire forming
a cross: such a symbol of
integration. Vertical and horizontal
the vine became divine.
Such a sight makes one wonder
how often we miss the
wholly Holy in a simple
climb of a morning glory?

Be Well

So love the sound and symbol
of well and well. One is a
source of sustenance, cleansing,
healing, i.e. wellness. It is
also a circular symbol of completeness.
Its holeness is a resource
for wholeness. Quench thirst,
clean wounds, the water from
the deep source is resource.
Spring, springs forth a fountain,
a reservoir of new life: wellness.
Hale, hearty, well, healthy
you be well.

Natural, Nature, Nurtures

Just then she ordered a
fried chicken and a waffle.
I have never seen her before and
I suspect never again. Her
sunglasses are pulled back on
her head. Her hair seems a
day too dirty. She is alone.
I am not attracted to her
except in her confident
solitude. This is not about
her, but how her natural
nature nurtures my need
to be authentic. Never be-
fore, never again, but always
a reminder of how perfect
it is to be imperfect. And,
to wonder how a chicken and
waffle tastes, at a small
bar/breakfast place in the
morning. Glory!

Rhyme

I do not write poems that rhyme.
It is difficult to find a word
that rhymes with rhyme.
    (It takes time.)

To take the time to rhyme
is not exactly a crime,
but sometimes it seems contrived.
    (This is where I arrived.)

In Ireland, I awoke to a gray day
on Galloway Bay. That line
came without thought and
    (wrought with rhyme.)

Ecstasy to find an authentic
rhyme and let it flow,
from where it comes is sublime
    (sometimes I write poems that rhyme.)

Coming

Today is the first Sunday of
Advent. 'Tis not the season
to be jolly." This is a timorous
season, for fear of the respon-
sibility that comes with the
coming—such a feminine
sense of gestation. The hen
broods the egg in the nest.
So too, this season of creative
brooding. We await that
which is to come. We also
fear the labor and pain of new
birth. Where there is birth, there
is blood. Let us not rush
around the labor, pain and
cost to the gift and grace
of the coming of the Cosmic
Christ.

Scurry

So in a simple scene I saw
a squirrel scamper along
the top of a wall. The con-
crete provided a path for
the dynamic scurry of the
squirrel. You who seek the
metaphor, let me reveal
what I saw. The static
provides the path for the
dynamic. In this vision,
scurry doesn't mean hurry.
It means to move along the
known seeking the unknown.
For there is the new that we knew
awaited us for the next
phase of our journey.
So in conclusion, I must
say, the scurrying squirrel
sought his store for the
winter and moved me.

Roll and Role

I am on a roll. When that
occurs, I go with the well-
known flow. Like a rolling
stone, just me, my journal,
a pencil and gathering no
moss, I let the poem find
its place: paper and pencil.

When on a roll there is no
role, just get myself out
of the way. Let it roll.
Speak of dreams, flowers,
weather, grandchildren,
just photograph with words,
record a scene, seen.

When I am on a roll, get
the hell out of the way,
cause this daydream is
the Vox Deo, or the grandiose
inflated sense that my roll
is no more than a self
delusional role of pretense.

Snow Dust, Star Dust

Today I awoke with an oxymoron:
a Texas snow. In fact it was
a dust of snow, with white remnants
on roof, lawn and car, no real
accumulation except in imagination.

Our desire for seasonal affirmation
inflates snow dust to star
dust. Such is the human de-
sire to make nature romantic.
So she is, until she shuts down

human traffic of roads, schools,
work, and transportation.
Her capricious presence posits
the polarities. We love her
artistic painting of the landscape.

We are victims of her vicious
overwhelming of human nature
by Mother Nature and at
the sometime healed by her mother
nature. So it is. Two things

are true at once: snow dust is
poetic. Snow storm is pathetic.
One empowers, the other over
powers. Who says, "you can't
have it both ways?"

Boat and Float

So, I sit on a chilly Friday
afternoon, journal in hand,
blank page awaiting a profound
word found in the ease of a
free day. Then in a sudden
moment of movement, a
bus hurries by. It is a floating
carrier of land and water. That
which rolls also floats. Here
in a moment on a chilly
Friday we see the possibility
that, that which might sink,
might float. The metaphor
is not overwhelming but
a reminder of the constant
paradox of polarities. So pleased,
on a chilly Friday, I don't have
a sinking feeling. I don't
float, but I don't fear the
deep. Depth is a metaphor
not a fact—unless one is
in a boat that won't float.

I See

So what's the deal with teal?
I read today about a scene that
had within something seen as teal.
How do I feel about teal? First
it is not on my spectrum—color
that is. I am so thankful for the subtle
nuance of the green/blue combo of
the two. I am told the word
describes the bird which pre-
sents with a stripe on it
that is the blue/green scene.
Teal. Teal, now we know,
teal is a bird, and we need
to see teal in the subtle, sub-
lime scene, seen in the spectrum
of our sensorium. Since
we sense teal, let us be not
blind to the real deal:
Teal. I see.

Novelty

Somehow in my personality,
I enjoy reverse sayings.
Such as: "There is no present
like the time." Or, "Two
knights passing in the ship."

Humor and irony are
divine, novelty. Novelty
means new. I knew
this, so it is old business,
but it is some of your business.

None of your business is
minding one's own
when I write I pray for novelty.
Finding a new way to say the old,
is the poet's way to say

it is always all of our
      business.

Who Knows?

I do not dread death. We will
be delivered from the laborious
laws of gravity: a three
dimensional universal
formula, having to bathe
and shave; having to
eliminate and sleep. So
when final sleep comes our
dreams end outside and
in. We are integrated in-
to the whole. Our anxiety
is alleviated, our identity is
irrelevant, our pain is no
more

or not. Who knows?

Entelechy

Entelechy is the inner principle
of energy that guides a person
to his/her potential. It is a
drive, a call to search and seek
that true, authentic, autonomous
being one was created to be.

It is the key to soul making.
Have you never been told to
honor your entelechy?
You now have. Seek the con-
scious concept to conceive the
concept that you were to become at

your conception. Don't you
hate it when you are patron-
zed in a poem?

Implore/Explore

Eliot implores us to
explore, at the end of
which we will "arrive
where we started and
know the place for the first
time." What changed? Place
or person? Dynamic means
power or motion. It is
the opposite of static.
Ecstasy means ex-stasis,
out of the static. If
one seeks the ecstatic
one must leave the known
and seek the unknown
to know it for the first
time. It seems all are
called, few choose.
Whether one chooses
or not, we are all summoned
to make the journey; we
are implored to ex-
plore.

CPSIA information can be obtained
at www.ICGtesting.com
Printed in the USA
LVHW112246180319
611097LV00001B/298/P

9 781942 956563